Sea Turtles Circle

PATRICIA GLEICHAUF

Illustrated by
KAREN STASZKO

PAGE PUBLISHING, INC.
New York, NY

First originally published by Page Publishing, Inc. 2019

ISBN 978-1-64544-805-1 (Paperback)
ISBN 978-1-64544-807-5 (Hardcover)
ISBN 978-1-64544-806-8 (Digital)

Printed in the United States of America

To Jack,

For an amazing forty years! Here's to many more!

A mama sea turtle lays her eggs in the sand. Never in the water, always on land.

She climbs up the beach in the dark of night so she won't be distracted by people or lights.

Then finds a good spot at the foot of a dune and builds her nest by the light of the moon.

She buries her eggs in a hole she dug deep. Her focus is her babies, their safety to keep.

After covering her nest with a ton of sand, she crawls back to the water away from the land.

For about sixty days, the babies live inside their eggs. It takes a long time to grow bodies and legs.

They are born with an egg tooth on their face.
It helps break their shell when they have outgrown
their space.

Sea turtle nests are protected from predators that threaten their well-being.

Volunteers walk the beach daily to look for nests and report what they are seeing.

It is called pipping when the babies break out of their eggs.

Then they rest for a day to stretch their necks and legs.

Their climb to the top of the nest is a very long reach before they scramble quickly across the beach.

Moonlight guides the hatchlings to the ocean. It is the only light there should be. Any other lights will lead them away from the sea.

When they reach the water, they swim very fast.

Committing their birth beach in their memory to last.

The hatchlings swim a long way to seagrass pastures where they can feed on plants and a little bit of meat.

Insects, shrimp and jelly fish are some of their favorite treats.

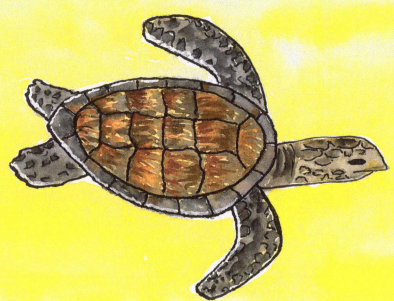

Before long, the hatchlings become juveniles. They have grown larger, and their swimming has become much stronger.

Their larger size keeps them safer. They can dive deeper and stay down longer.

Hawksbill Turtle
Most colorful turtle, has a narrow beak and a long neck.

Flatback Turtle
Has a flat, smooth shell and is located only in Australia.

Kemp's Ridley Turtle
The smallest sea turtle, has a circular shell, some nest during the day in a group.

Olive Ridley Turtle
Most abundant sea turtle, some nest during the day in a group.

There are seven types of sea turtles; each has its own name.

Green Turtle
Fastest-swimming sea turtle, has a teardrop-shaped shell.

Loggerhead Turtle
Slowest-swimming sea turtle with a very large head.

Leatherback Turtle
World's largest sea turtle; each has a pink spot on its head.

They are each a little different, but mostly, they're the same.

When needing to feel safer, land turtles and pond turtles can pull their heads and legs inside their shells.

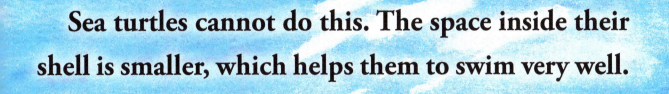

Sea turtles cannot do this. The space inside their shell is smaller, which helps them to swim very well.

You might see a sea turtle peeking its head out of the ocean to breathe before diving to the bottom to forage and feed.

Sea turtles' eyes are always crying, but they are not always sad. Tears wash salt from their bodies. Too much salt can be very bad.

Juvenile turtles spend their time swimming the world's oceans. They swim, and they swim; they go and go and go! As they are swimming, they grow and grow and grow!

Male turtles will not return to land for any reason. Female turtles will leave salt water only during nesting season.

Many years later, when they are fully grown, sea turtles begin finding their way back home.

There the circle begins once more, building her nest on her own birth shore.

A mama sea turtle lays her eggs in the sand. Never in the water, always on land.

About the Author

Pat Gleichauf lives in Upstate New York with her husband, Jack. Writing for children is her dream come true. She is dedicated to children's literacy, and her goal is to "hook kids on books." Pat doesn't miss an opportunity to read her books to students at schools and libraries. She uses this time to encourage children to follow their dreams.

This is the third book in her *Under the Sea* series. Her first book in the series, *Horses of the Sea*, was awarded a gold medal by the Florida Authors and Publishers Association in 2018. *Starfish Gazing*, won second place in the Purple Dragonfly international children's book competition in 2019.

About the Illustrator

Karen Staszko has been creating beautiful watercolor paintings for thirty years. She studied watercolor painting for seventeen years and has been teaching it for ten years. Originally from Colchester, Connecticut, Karen recently moved to North Ridgeville, Ohio, with her husband, Meron, to live closer to their daughter and grandson. They also lived for eleven years in Southwest Florida. Karen loves art in any form. Her passion is helping beginner artists create beautiful paintings.

Printed in the USA
CPSIA information can be obtained
at www.ICGtesting.com
LVHW060924290224
772793LV00007B/6